LOVE IS A DOG THAT BITES WHEN IT'S SCARED

Also by Courtney Marie Andrews

Old Monarch

LOVE IS A DOG THAT BITES WHEN IT'S SCARED

Courtney Marie Andrews

Love Is a Dog That Bites When It's Scared
copyright © 2025 by Courtney Marie Andrews. All rights reserved.
Printed in China. No part of this book may be used or reproduced
in any manner whatsoever without written permission except in
the case of reprints in the context of reviews.

Andrews McMeel Publishing
a division of Andrews McMeel Universal
1130 Walnut Street, Kansas City, Missouri 64106

www.andrewsmcmeel.com

25 26 27 28 29 TEN 10 9 8 7 6 5 4 3 2 1

ISBN: 978-1-5248-9387-3

Library of Congress Control Number: 2024950929

Illustrations by Courtney Marie Andrews

Editor: Patty Rice
Art Director/Designer: Julie Barnes
Production Editor: Dave Shaw
Production Manager: Julie Skalla

Andrews McMeel Publishing is committed to the responsible
use of natural resources and is dedicated to understanding,
measuring, and reducing the impact of our products on the
natural world. By choosing this product, you are supporting
responsible management of the world's forests. The FSC®
label means that the materials used for this product come
from well-managed FSC®-certified forests, recycled materials,
and other controlled sources.

ATTENTION: SCHOOLS AND BUSINESSES
Andrews McMeel books are available at quantity discounts with
bulk purchase for educational, business, or sales promotional use.
For information, please e-mail the Andrews McMeel Publishing
Special Sales Department: sales@andrewsmcmeel.com.

**LOVE IS
A DOG
THAT BITES
WHEN IT'S
SCARED**

PUPPY LOVE

THE SUMMER EVERYTHING
SMELLED OF MAGNOLIAS

Not honey, nor maple, but *sweet*.
We walked windswept, sniffing.
Salt air shaken and stirred
—a hurricane teasing the island.

That is the moment I'll come back to
thumbing through my memory Rolodex.
Absent words exposing
only what was felt.

Not everything owned is tangible.
Not everything tangible is owned.
It's better when it's not kept or borrowed
but uniquely present.

A human heart is there, beating.
Isn't that enough? A whiff, a color,
a dream, a life bending
toward another sunset.

Wrapped in a quilt brighter
than the public, we sought ideas
bigger than ourselves.
We found love that summer,

the summer everything smelled of magnolias.

ORANGES

When there is nothing to do, we eat oranges.
On our backs, belly-up, citrus quenching
our pain. Rumi speaks of God,
but had he ever tried a Florida fruit
fresh from the vine?
What a privilege to find nothing to do
for one hour in the day!
To laze about like two koalas,
eucalyptus smiles,
sour-pressed lips,
rolling around the orchard,
dirt in our teeth.

THIS IS MY BIRD

Ibis, Spoonbill
Honeyeater, Lorikeet
all mate for life.

Ruffling feathers,
free and flying,
always returning.

We could be
collecting branches
for mi casa,

you in the sky,
me here in this tree,
or vice versa?

Meanwhile, every stranger
assumes unbound pleasure,
unmoored autonomy.

Yet, we find our way back.

ENOUGH

"How much?" we asked.
More than the ocean?
The sky? The trees?
More than our history?

Enough to stop the comet
from crashing into Earth?
Enough to keep trying?
Enough to risk failure?

Enough to crawl
out of any debris,
lifting our pasts up
from the rubbish?

More than words,
knowledge?
More than explanations?
Bodies? Time?

ACCIDENTS

I did not set out in search, some lonely excavator.
There was abundance, a *gold* mine of security.
Though the real stuff falls like rain. All of the sudden
you are wet, remembering that umbrella
in the downstairs closet,
so comforting and safe,
but always forgotten.
Meanwhile, the storm stains your Italian pink suede
and for the first time in years you feel it *all*.
Accidents happen.
You drop the wine bottle, aisle eight. It shatters,
cuts your hand. Some cashier
is rushing toward you with a broom.
You call your mother to tell her what happened.
She is worried because she remembers
how hurt you were in your early twenties.
You assure her *that* cut was different.
Your lover arrives, peering over the mess.
He's afraid too,
because love is like holding up a mirror
and looking at the most terrifying parts of yourself.
Shattered glass, messy beginnings.
The timing is god-awful.
Your gut is a shy announcer.
Yet, there you are,
sitting on the curb in a puddle,
laughing, bleeding.

WHAT MAKES YOUR LOVER CRY

- Singing "Auld Lang Syne" at midnight
- Lights on Evergreens, twinkling little beauties
- Strangers kissing unpretentiously
- Curly yellow dogs
- Time running out
- Couples dancing badly
- Small surprises
- Children singing off-key
- The view at the top of Dreamy Draw
- Future nostalgia
- Dreams, always dreams
- Sleeping seals
- Vince Guaraldi piano
- The Pacific
- Most likely every ocean
- People staring at water
- Stylish old folks at airports
- Long letters
- Flowers, picked, bought, or untainted
- Unexpected visits
- Magnolias, Weeping Willows
- Saguaro and Mesquite, especially at dusk
- Falling asleep talking
- Believing in someone

A REQUEST FOR BRAVERY

Fetch me a coat, the thrifted one
with turquoise patches fraying.
Radiate your humor with heat.
Imperfectly charming.
We are laughing at the red devil,
agreeing he represents love,
ropes, laces, glue, thread. People
find daring ways to stick together,
to stay warm in the winter.

Between verses I drop hints
—a call to action for extravagence,
scavenger hunts, rabbits
in magic hats. Unexpected
nectar. Surprise sweetness.
I don't care if happiness is for fools.
I double-dog dare you
to fly out to meet me,
to risk it all.

FIRST TIME

Love me like the first time,
as if your heart has never been
umbilically wrapped around another's.
No damage from yesterday.
Nothing to climb up from
—a time when you were a sparrow
building possible futures
from youth's masonry.
No more therapy.
Love me like a puppy,
like a child,
like a monk,
like you believe
in nothing going wrong.

BIRTHDAY CAKE

One misleading candle
stuck in the sweet icing.
You watched me blow it out,
my austere last-night lips
quivering years.
I wondered if you
could see my wish
—*a prayer* to not grow
a day older alone.

OUR STREET

Will you follow me there?
To the dead-end street
that is commitment?
Our house will be
the charming one on the block.
"It has character,"
they will say.
A little crooked,
but one of a kind.
Unconventional,
yet safe and still.
I promise I won't grow cilantro
in the garden.
Only tulips, my love,
and a Japanese maple.
The bikes won't rust.
We will ride them often.
I will sing in the mornings
while you're still sleeping, my love.
Songs about us,
loved ones too.
You'll play piano at night
as I fall asleep
and we will both agree,
"It's about time
we get this thing tuned."

HEART SEDIMENT/SENTIMENTS:
California

When I think of us, I think of Sonoma. Under the
Californian sun—a blazing orange in the vineyard.
I have memorized every color: the algae, pine cone,
dried moss, the golden yellow. I think of the bed,
the way the sheets tucked tightly around my body.
Unspoken cocoon. The night was ours, but tomorrow
would belong to so many. When we got to San Diego,
I sat next to the lonely seal, yawning, rolling away
from the tourists. The seal embodied the morning, our
parting. You took my picture as I cried. You like when
I feel because it makes you feel free. There was, of
course, "the kiss" in Salt Lake City under the Rabbit
moon on that sterile kitchen floor, hesitant of the love
we contained. If only our falling could be as clean as
that floor. Can we take that kiss back? I love California
too much. I'm a *West Coast person*. It didn't suit us
and the timing was off. When I think of us, I think of
San Francisco sea glass, Leavenworth in the blizzard,
Seattle in the taxi, Vancouver in the icy rain and the
silly way we stared too long and you'd ask "What?"
as if you didn't understand why we were falling.
When I think of us, I think of tomorrow more than
yesterday because love will do that to you. You start
imagining California forever and every other place
disintegrates into the rearview.

LOVE IS AN ANIMAL WITH A FEVER

You want me to pretend
we did not roll around,
thumbing our paged bodies
across that dramatic bed,
pencils in our teeth,
twisted in a towel at the
edge, as if our feelings
did not involve
the lives of anyone else
but the pretty swan.
But darling, love
is an animal with a fever.
We are two sick martyrs
exchanging glances.
Paris is cold.
You are telling me
to quit smoking,
as if I will live forever
alongside you.
I am a terrible actress,
unable to hide my cough.
Will the world ever know?
Or will I die from the fever?

WINDOWS

Staring at the freckle in your eye,
the shape of your childhood home.
I see it so clearly now.
You, once afraid to let me in.

Now your eyes are windows
that I kiss open in the summer,
like a dog licking St. Roch's wounds.

Curtained to strangers passing,
I make myself at home,
smitten in privacy and closeness,
unafraid of what I see in you.

BUTTERFLY EFFECT

I could be in London
sitting at your Hackney table,
but I am here in Chicago
watching the bloated sun
rise behind the skyline.

IMPATIENCE

Scrambling an egg on the stove.
Watching the edges cling,
how the onions wedge in fear
of being swallowed.

An Easter color palette
blurring together like
a post-impressionist painting
—a misunderstood morning.

Pouring grinds into the French press.
The boiling water, the impatience
of pressing down
right away.

Eagerness is a family trait.
Sometimes I skip pages in good books.
Sometimes I cut airport lines
and act aloof when attendants notice.

The coffee *is watered down*.
We can miss the purest essence
of *the thing* in attempt
to experience it sooner.

As a matter of fact,
nothing about this morning
tastes or feels right.
You haven't called yet.

The eggs are burning.

SEA-FOAM

The moon is a paper
with a tiny note ripped from it,
where I scribble my grievances
and mail them away.
You are like the sea-foam sticking to the wave,
lazy and afraid to melt into me.
I am the wave, reeling in and out
attempting change.
There is nothing worse than a brave fool.
The sea oats sway in laughter at us,
our exhausting games of getting stuck
and breaking free. They are rooted
in their freedom, dancing in the ground.
We reach for them,
only to recede at low tide.

JUPITER HOTEL

Slip into my bed
—a familiar space.
Courtyard crawl,
night noises echoing,
West Coast brine.
All the sacred pain
of change.

Slip in
with morning malaise.
These vows,
these conversations.
Like a machine,
we make the choice
to repair what is broken.

Slip in
and kiss me
like James Dean returning.
While the world crumbles,
while Portland pines,
while we recoil.

Let us try again.

HEART SEDIMENT/SENTIMENTS:
Santa Fe

I thought Santa Fe might offer me some direction. Some crooked tree bent toward an ideal. At the El Rey Hotel I point out the moon to Boramie before singing "Dublin Blues." The smoke of the campfire rises, dimming my certainty—a flashlight running out of batteries. But who needs answers when they only lead to more questions? The Palo Verde yawns. I relate to the exhausting desire for survival or love. Maybe those two are one and the same. Maybe people can die because their love runs out. Maybe I've died a thousand times before.

When the Navajo see an owl it's an omen. They look for clues in the sky or sand. I wait. Wait until my heart is bursting. You can only mend yourself so many times before you feel comfortable with what is broken.

There is an old man in a caramel poncho falling asleep in his drink. His wife rubs his back, helps him to bed. There is love, *still.*

It does not have a pointer finger or an owl or an arrow. Its existence is not an answer, only a question we never have to ask.

DUSK

A glimmer of sadness creeps in with dusk. The sky becomes a bruise, tender with impermanence. For a moment I become needy for previous hours. Roanoke looks pretty in pink, like a little doll, blushing. How can pretty things feel so sad? In tall shadows of the hills I begin to long for moments I found meaningless while they were happening; bikes crashing into each other, airport arrivals, love songs in bad keys. At daybreak these brevities become a balloon whose ribbon I'm chasing after—a place between chapters I cannot grasp, an uneasy time between the end and the beginning.

TAKE ME TO THE ZOO

The couples in this fancy restaurant look sad
with their turtlenecks and golden earrings.
There must be something funny enough
to spit out their wine for.
Or something interesting enough to speak of.

At the zoo the lions and chimpanzees
roar or scream with passion.
These animals,
so full of desire, rage, fire,
so unafraid of feeling.
Such an urgency to survive.

We sit silent at dinner.
In the taxi home
I stick my face out the window
and yell into the wind.

THE PRICE OF LOVE

It was when I saw Una
crying at the moon,
similar to the one
she lost him on,
that I finally understood
the price of love.
Wrapped in her sister's arms
shelling out a grief tax,
the high cost
for years of union.
My greeting stirred her sorrow.
All I could offer was a meek apology.

How cheap sorry sounds now
as I lay here in Columbus
staring at the cloudy sky.

PARAKEET

This is what it feels like to be a woman
whose heart is captured.
Think of the flamboyant parakeet
squawking in a cage,
only let out every other day
to fly and sing.

Once I would happily hum,
naked in your uncertainty.
Now, I rustle my feathers,
expand my chest,
search for the door.

HUMOROUS DETOURS

You laugh

as if it's not happening.
As if I am
Elizabeth Taylor singing

"Send in the Clowns."

Locusts lament
their song.
This autumn night
under trees undressing.

My hope is deafening
with your humorous detours.
Laugh, my love,
then say you are drunk.

Pass conversations
off to the morning,
while each day
the sunrise grows tired.

SULKING STRAYS

THEY SAY IT'S SUMMER

Lying in St. James
mimicking the lilies,
freckles popping up
as permanent reminders
of this bittersweet summer.

I'm soaking it in,
this grief that has nowhere to travel,
this love that has no place to rest.
I feel both happy and sad,
both old and young,
both brave and afraid,
both sure and unsure.

An elderly couple whistles
under the canopy.
There are two swans mating.
There are willows swaying.
The world is a beautiful classroom
with pain as our teacher.

CAR KEYS

Losing words
as if they were car keys
or a debit card at the bar.

As if I can call up the waitress
and ask her to hold on to them,
retrieve them in the morning.

Moments pass,
the igniting conversations
fizz out like fireworks.

You leave the room.
    I am silent
when words can start the engine.

WHAT'S SO FUNNY?

Eager to have you completely
I left before you could
beat me to the punchline.

IMAGINATION

Can I fill the void
watching old couples
walk in rhythm
on the cobblestone?
Is that enough
to fill my heart
with your absence?
How perfectly sad,
these lamplit streets.
Doughy gloom rolling
in late July,
the romance and mystery.
Colors in a picture I can
no longer paint.
I keep you here
—a wishful penny
I am saving
for the right fountain.
Warming my pocket
with scenes from a town
where I am only a stranger.

ARIZONA GIRL

It is eight degrees in Chicago
and you call to tell me
we must continue to be friends.

Men in parkas
scrape ice off the sidewalk.
The ground is a black hole.

You can see the couple's breaths,
expanding toward each other.

I am quiet as this block,

where little snowflakes
shimmer in the streetlight
and stick to the metal.

I don't have the right jacket
to receive your cold outlook.
Not after all we have shared.

LOVE IS A DOG THAT BITES WHEN IT'S SCARED

HEART SEDIMENT/SENTIMENTS:
Joshua Tree

Strangers at the bar once felt our love. So much so they tried
to screw me with their eyes or words.
That's the problem with what is unrequited,
everyone thinks they can own what they feel in the air.

Now at this hokey western bar, I am carelessly
wedged between two couples.
Do poets want what's unattainable
so they can feed longing to the hungry world?

There is no love bouncing off me.
The bartender forgets to bring the bill.

EVERYWHERE

It's the places I go.
My failed attempts to separate
you from them,
the beauty or reverence.
The sand I find
from France
sticks to everything.
Your heart is a permanent marker
bleeding into all I do.
Mexico or Tortola,
the beach you refused
to wear sandals on.
Your flaws like a snag
pulling two fabrics closer.
I wander the forgettable alleys
and remember your clothes.

HEARTBROKEN IN NOTTINGHAM

There was a beautiful woman crying
in a pew at St. Peter's
with her emerald dress, pearls,
absolutely hysterical.
No one bothered her
but a bird caught in the rafter
with a menacing desire to escape.

I am not seeking God here
but I believe every human spirit
is made of similar stuff.
Familiar sorrow,
recognizable joy.
To share a pew with lives so distinct,
to reach for the sky after falling.

HEARTBROKEN IN WALES

Like a little lamb
with a brightly colored tag
I knew what was coming. Still
I greenly went about my days
grazing and fattening.

For a time, denial was a
pasture on the horizon.
Fields of flowers and grass,
such pretty distractions,
but captive hearts
still get slaughtered.

PROVINCETOWN

I want to go back to Provincetown
where salt sticks to everything.
Where the dream of us still flickers
in that old house on Main Street.
The two men running the inn
felt sorry for me.
They knew I wasn't meant
to be coming alone.
They sent up two plates.
I didn't eat either.
Outside, a lovely drag queen
on a bicycle, a proposal,
a baker laughing,
the gardens, immaculate.
Pastels and pasties.
I waltzed out like a ghost,
gray in a technicolor world,
wanting to feel a part
of those happy endings.
The cosplay psychic
promised the dream of us
was still alive
and I was able to go on
for a few more days.

NEW ORLEANS

Flowers in the window,
antique spoons,
beaver moon,
loud brass bands,
corn husk bouquets,
eggs-easy,
affordable Chagall,
side-street kisses.
Love marked me
in this place.

UNDER THE OAK

You know how the abandoned dog
keeps returning to the place he was left?

I keep walking back to the oak
    Sitting in the oak
        Swinging from the oak
And you never retrieve me.

FALLEN OBJECTS

I didn't believe in ghosts
until heartache cast me
tailing into the public library
of my history.

Love, I know, so capable of
dangerous illusions.
Still, when the flour
mysteriously falls from the shelf

I prepare for your return.

MASTERPIECE

Silence is a great storyteller.
Better than Shakespeare
or Hemingway.

Your refusal to speak
elicits my greatest works
of tragedy and comedy.

SULKING STRAYS

To think we are now
two wayfaring pups
once in the home
we called love.

UNSOLICITED ADVICE FROM STRANGERS

Vanisha, Freehand Hotel:

Karma, baby, karma.

Tammy, Wilburn Tavern:

Wait for the love you deserve.

Ellen the Red Witch, Fortune Teller Bar:

Ask the mirror.

Peri, Waccabuc, New York:

What is meant for you
will find its way to you.

HEART SEDIMENT/SENTIMENTS:
Wellfleet

The last time we kissed was the first time I cooked you dinner.
You pretended to love it, even though
the noodles were undercooked.

What do I make of your departure?
I cannot cook and I do not have anyone
to lie to me about it.

THREE PSYCHICS

So much money spent
on wonder.
One said you were
trying to get yourself back.
Another said you were
trying to get me back.
Another said
I should try
and get myself back.
And at the end
of each phone call
only me
and a dial tone.

SPACE BETWEEN WHAT'S FELT

A postcard from Sky Harbor.
Directions to Mexico.
A moonstone scavenged
from Cambria.
Is there anything more devastating
than a love letter unsent?
Those little words hanging in midair
as its receiver waits unknowingly
with thoughts of her own
and flowers from Italy,
a Skyliner's song, that silk dress.
Three stamps for international travel
with those little mysterious words
Somewhere in Utah.

DIFFERENT STUFF

I would leave this bar
right now, but the heart
is a different organ.
It imagines the horse
and stands lassoing
the sky. Go on pride,
go on. There is no cure,
except maybe
time.

SEARCHING FOR LOVE AGAIN

Tracing a trail of roses
planted in a line
along Jones Beach.

They were not intended for me
but a girl can fantasize,
can wonder.

Peru, on the other side of the world,
those two dollar scratchers, God,
the dead, prisoners gambling.

Dreams of impossible things
breed life.
I follow the flowers.

MEG RYAN

Am I supposed to walk through Central Park
like I'm looking for love?
Tangled with Sparky the dog,
his owner forced to gentle his pace.

It's not gonna work. His calves say
he cares too much about fitness.
Plus, Sparky is incredibly
cliché.

Meg Ryan made me think
there's an apex to every story,
but maybe some people never reach
the happy ending.

Some people die in a kingdom of cats.
Some with jumbled puzzles for minds.
Fools like me think
love is what Meg Ryan promised us.

Listen, I just need to know
if I'm supposed
to walk down this aisle of benches,
or wait on the bench.

MY NORTHEASTERN STAR

Today, for the first time,
I went an entire hour without
your consideration.
Then you reappeared,
an elusive Northeastern star.
I was reminded of how slowly
light travels to its admirers.
Perhaps stars are also romantics gazing.
How quick we are to organize meaning
from patterns in the sky.
Some messages arrive too late.

THE SUN'LL COME OUT TOMORROW

Look, there!
across Manukau Harbour,
a fluorescent trail
of shimmering tomorrow,
a future beyond mistakes.
I have been so contained,
this heart chamber,
this wishing well
filled with copper,
this hope machine
once malfunctioning.
Now, ready to swim
from this sad shore.

ON/OFF

Come on out
and see what the world is all about.
There is love, still. Families
reuniting in airports. Cute old couples
dressed to impress in the museum.
Bird sounds, highway noise,
unexpected summer rain,
an old jukebox at Vaughn's
that is only one US dollar for five songs,
a laughing table of friends,
postcards, harmonies,
a chubby little groundhog
who sees his shadow,
a billion bad pool players
and even more bad dancers.
But the point is
everyone is trying their best.
Come on out. There are all kinds of faith,
serendipitous run-ins, films
to mirror our humanity,
Billie Holiday songs
and roads that lead places
we see differently next time.
And trees. So many trees. And they sway
and rustle and are bad dancers just like us.

REMEMBERING TO FORGET

I am beginning to forget your smile.
With lines deep as dry riverbeds,
sarcastically smirking, poking fun,
laughing like a coyote in heat.

I am beginning to forget your eyes.
The way you transposed the world.
Drawn like a moth to the light,
choosing a love song on every jukebox.

I am beginning to forget your touch.
Our warm bodies pressed like flowers
between pages. Opening
the journal where I wrote:

I will never forget you.

EXPECTATIONS AT THE ZOO

Courtney Marie Andrews

I DO NOT WANT TO WRITE ABOUT LOVE

What about my not-so-healthy breakfast
or the old mop that needs replacing?
Patsy Cline is skipping
"You made me love you . . ."

I curse, lifting the needle.
There is a groundhog in my garden again.
He is alone, content,
eating the winter weeds.

I'll talk about him! His adorably round belly.
He scurries when I open the door.
Guess I'll have to find another subject.
What about that man from Ecuador I kissed?

That wasn't love and he took great interest
in my pointless rock collection.
I told him a lie about studying archaeology.
Love doesn't lie, so that's safe to mention.

Distractions are good.
I draw a bath and regret the candle I light.
It smells like you, which leads me back.
So, I think about the old women.

They dress how they want
and drink boxed wine from the fridge.
English caramels, too.
Then they purse their lips and mention

their ex-husbands and wives.
Goddamn it.
Back to the mop!
I really need to get a new one.

SOLSTICE

It happens to be
the second longest day
of the year.
Not only in this hemisphere,
but also on the planet
that is my heart.
When you wait by the window as a child
you spend your life waiting.
The day is long
because no matter what I choose to fill it with
the antagonist never comes into view.
The day is long
because the sun won't set over Nairn
until nearly midnight.
The day is long because of the silence
with all its implications.
If I could tell the little girl in me
to walk outside
away from the window of expectation,
I would tie her shoes,
let her run free,
teach her how
to save herself.

MY LIFE

In the Highlands, Alan points out
the black patches on the Monroe.
"Controlled burn," he says.
They kill it off so it'll grow back stronger,
           more fertile.
What dies either leaves forever
or comes back with ferocity.
I make an ash angel
covering my entire body with soot.
I am the greenery moving through the black.
I am the daffodil sprouting from the smoke.
You broke my heart
and yet, I am alive.

DOLPHINS

Sometimes all you can do
is drive out to Topanga
and stare at the ocean
just to feel a direction.

THE REDUCTION OF MYSELF

For some time
I was a contortionist,
play-doh-ing
into plastic truths.

Squeezing into the jeans,
dimming light,
holding tongue,
yielding closeness.

On the lawn, Laney points out
a constellation
in the ebony sky.
I sneeze.

If you do not name yourself,
the world will.

CARVING

Trying to sharpen my mind
like a knife to a pencil.
Chisel away the excess,
hold myself accountable
for unnecessary hope.

EXPECTATIONS AT THE ZOO

Better to not
have expectations at the zoo.
The platypus might be sleeping,
the lion, tired of gawking children.
He might not call
or get on the plane,
but you can sit in the sunshine
and be glad you're not a caged eagle.

LOVE IS A DOG THAT BITES WHEN IT'S SCARED

HEART SEDIMENT/SENTIMENTS:
New York City

This Manhattan hotel bar has palms growing in pots
framing the window which makes me feel like the
romantic interest in *Casablanca*. Does anyone care
about anyone but themselves? A woman lights a
cigarette in the corner booth. Surely, the romance
does not go unnoticed? Her lover stares off,
                                                                removed.
Then the waiter tells her to put it out. *He* noticed.
These days only broken rules and isolated absurdity
are taken into account. I try to remain focused like
a predator inching in on its meal. That sounds intense,
but I feel we should aim for the tallest mountain
and hopefully make basecamp. Ever since I read an
article in the *New York Times* on attention spans,
I force myself to look up from this spinning wheel
of interruptions. We are convicts of distraction.

Courtney Marie Andrews

For a sweet minute I am awake, pressing the moment
like a leaf on the pavement, the audible crackling.

I do not want to live like a hangman waiting for vowels.

I want to feel it all! The subtle nuance of silverware
sounds, the lighting, the conversation. The love or
absence of love. Purgatory is its own kind of hell.
Apathy and detachment rest there. I want to look
a stranger in the eye with my whole self.
I want to light a cigarette, take it in.
I want to remember.

DIVING

Like a seagull
who dives headfirst
into salt water,
coming up short,

knowing below
in murky waters
a possible fish
—a promise.

The bird who is
basking on the rock
of longing.
The bird

who knows within,
diving is what propels
a lonely hunter
back into a soar.

ISLAND IMMUNITY

I want to be an island
—a self-sustaining slice of earth
where sailors crash on my shore.
Inevitable endings would be easier.
I could prepare for loneliness.
He has tools to mend his boat,
while I erode my shore with tears.
There are bigger worries
than heartbreak.
Like, abandoning yourself.
I have turned my pain into a place.
And yet, I cry when the sailor
fixes his rudder.

REPRESSED HEARTS

The silence will spin
a ball around your core
so tight, you can't breathe
or eat the pasta.

You cannot live long
with a feeling hiding.

THE DREAM

You want it to be like it was,
the innocence of unknowing.
Older, you purse your lips
and kiss someone
you do not know.
The "plenty of fish"
you were promised,
turn to algae on your line.
Canoe tips, a familiar voice,
the myth of "your" man.
Diving in the cold,
coming up for air,
only to find your own
reflection.
How it is now.

NECTAR OF LIFE

Grandma Dorothy stood at the kitchen sink
nearly every evening of her life
cleaning and watching the hummingbirds.
Small tragedies everywhere
with windows peering out to hope.
Do you know about the hummingbird's memory?
They can fly five-hundred miles in one go
remembering every part of their journey.
Dorothy stood staring
trying to forget.
I want to be the bird.
I want to be the lifeline.
For her
I want to be on the outside
flying toward sweetness.

NOVEMBER 2ND

It is Día de los Muertos.
I am walking alongside
my dead grandmother.

Her red scarf,
an afterlife soliloquy.
Skeletons laugh around me.

The women are so pretty
dressed in dried flowers
kissing their children.

Wheels of the parade
hobble, caress life
but what of her ceased heart?

Does it still work
long after the lungs
refused to push air?

We cannot see
tomorrow's joy,
what inspires survival.

Canvas-faced drummers
paint thunder
on a street named Desire.

NO EXAMPLE

Wooden box of rings;
moonstone, emerald, topaz.
Representing some birth
or self-recognition, but none
a committed gesture.
No born from an embrace
or passion or trust.
No learned unity
in my own household,
only how to grieve
behind closed doors,
dressed in silver.

LITTLE GIRLS

see boundless love
in the eyes of each
imaginary prince
when they should be shown
an imperfect horse
with a human, trying.

BELIEVING

Suzanne looks unconcerned
stirring her pointer finger
in her tea.

"Who needs true love?
As we get older
companionship is enough."

I wince, burning my tongue.
Her partner of many years
sits near, gossiping about town.

They do not touch,
kiss,
or stare.

I die a little inside
like a child discovering
their mother is the real St. Nick.

Hours pass, we toss paint.
I draw you on a throne.
Suzanne paints an empty house.

The gods are tragic comedians.
"Why do you concern yourself
with longing?"

Because how else do we
continue on?
Living is believing.

MORNINGS WITH JUDY

Paper clippings litter the floor.
Insulation rot, leaky roof,
but the garden is intact.
Yes, the agaves
spring up like cannons.

She has house paint
on her Goodwill sweater.
Her slight figure towers
humbly, a distortion that requires
listening to her quiet authority.

She looks past my eyes
and says people need too much.
"That's why the world is sad and sick.
The need eats them . . .
makes them crazy."

I circle my finger in breadcrumbs
wondering how my future will unfold,
suddenly needing her to explain
how to exsist as simply as a flower
in its bed,

happy to be anything at all.

ANGELS AND SAINTS

Angel of love, saint of marriage.
Strings, flutes, guitars, flying
little hanging reminders.

Angel of poetry, saint of creativity.
Muses, robes, gallantry, color,
our reflections in pines.

Maria opens the register,
peering in adoration
at the wooden angel

in my hands. Miracles,
she sings. Miracles,
wonderful miracles.

Courtney Marie Andrews

EMBROIDERED STARS

How can you judge a star?
Suspended, bending time,
a pinhole into what was
and what will be.
Combusting, forming flesh
that is your sister or brother
in Hong Kong or Kilkenny.
A part of the star that made us
wants to go to war.
Isn't it ridiculous?
How can you sever the bond,
the seam that threads
the embroidered heart?
How can you kill
a part of yourself
and stand proud
looking up at the sky?

COME VISIT

I am an ambassador of love.
These towns with their similar shapes,
streets filling and emptying by early morning.
Have you heard, kind stranger?
Love is a beautiful place,
even with its messy alleys
and poor city planning.
Come get lost.
Do not let possible endings
keep you from it.
Visit it sometime
when you are most afraid of yourself.

With love, cma.

INDEX

A REQUEST FOR BRAVERY	15
ACCIDENTS	13
ANGELS AND SAINTS	82
ARIZONA GIRL	39
BELIEVING	80
BIRTHDAY CAKE	17
BUTTERFLY EFFECT	22
CAR KEYS	36
CARVING	68
COME VISIT	84
DIFFERENT STUFF	54
DIVING	72
DOLPHINS	66

DUSK	27
EMBROIDERED STARS	83
ENOUGH	12
EVERYWHERE	41
EXPECTATIONS AT THE ZOO	69
FALLEN OBJECTS	47
FIRST TIME	16
HEART SEDIMENT/SENTIMENTS: *California*	19
HEART SEDIMENT/SENTIMENTS: *Joshua Tree*	40
HEART SEDIMENT/SENTIMENTS: *New York City*	70
HEART SEDIMENT/SENTIMENTS: *Santa Fe*	26
HEART SEDIMENT/SENTIMENTS: *Wellfleet*	51
HEARTBROKEN IN NOTTINGHAM	42
HEARTBROKEN IN WALES	43
HUMOROUS DETOURS	31

I DO NOT WANT TO WRITE ABOUT LOVE	63
IMAGINATION	38
IMPATIENCE	23
ISLAND IMMUNITY	73
JUPITER HOTEL	25
LITTLE GIRLS	79
LOVE IS AN ANIMAL WITH A FEVER	20
MASTERPIECE	48
MEG RYAN	56
MORNINGS WITH JUDY	81
MY LIFE	65
MY NORTHEASTERN STAR	57
NECTAR OF LIFE	76
NEW ORLEANS	45
NO EXAMPLE	78

NOVEMBER 2ND	77
ON/OFF	59
ORANGES	10
OUR STREET	18
PARAKEET	30
PROVINCETOWN	44
REMEMBERING TO FORGET	60
REPRESSED HEARTS	74
SEA-FOAM	24
SEARCHING FOR LOVE AGAIN	55
SOLSTICE	64
SPACE BETWEEN WHAT'S FELT	53
SULKING STRAYS	49
TAKE ME TO THE ZOO	28
THE DREAM	75

THE PRICE OF LOVE	29
THE REDUCTION OF MYSELF	67
THE SUMMER EVERYTHING SMELLED OF MAGNOLIAS	9
THE SUN'LL COME OUT TOMORROW	58
THEY SAY IT'S SUMMER	35
THIS IS MY BIRD	11
THREE PSYCHICS	52
UNDER THE OAK	46
UNSOLICITED ADVICE FROM STRANGERS	50
WHAT MAKES YOUR LOVER CRY	14
WHAT'S SO FUNNY?	37
WINDOWS	21